Rog!
To my
I love y

MW01288677

Roland.

FIND PEACE

One POP at a Time

ROLAND GRIFFITH

Acknowledgements

I am indebted to Tim Anderson, who introduced me to his writers group, and over numerous cups of coffee, encouraged me to help others by writing about my journey.

Thank you to Paula Peters for her coaching and to Jan Phillips for reducing a massive pile of words into an understandable narrative. Thanks to Laurie Chipman for providing the illustrations, and to Jacquie Stenger for my professional mug shot.

Thanks to Gordon Kessler for his valuable expertise and direction; to Kelly Ludden for her great design and formatting work; and special thanks to Julie Tenenbaum for her extraordinary editing.

Cover and Book Design by Kelly Ludden Design

ISBN-13: 978-1500615659

ISBN-10: 150061565X

To Connie,
my wife and best friend,
who planted the seed
that flowered into this book.

Table of Contents

Chapter 1
Introduction

*Because I was determined to overcome the depression that had held me prisoner for so long, I developed a systematic and motivating method that accelerated my process of **breaking free**.*

Chapter 1

Introduction

For many years, I lived with depression. I was uncomfortable in my own skin. I was often afraid to express my opinions, even around friends. I thought I was missing something that other people seemed to have. Even though my life felt empty, incomplete, and burdensome, I wanted to look and act as if it were perfect. I felt imprisoned by the problems life continually presented me. When I looked into the future, I saw only more problems I would have to solve. There was nothing to look forward to: nothing exciting, nothing fulfilling, and certainly nothing like joy. I had no hope that life could be anything different than what I was experiencing. I was stuck.

Today, my life is full of hope and joy. I look forward to waking up every morning because every day is a good day, full of things I love to do: drinking my first cup of coffee, talking with my buddies, working on projects in the yard and around the house, playing golf, traveling with my wife, and being with my family. Life is exciting.

Oddly enough, I did all of those things while I was depressed, but it's different now. I have a sense of freedom, and the future is full of possibilities. I'm not concerned about how I appear to others or how they might judge me. I am not so critical of others or myself. I can express myself openly, which would have been impossible before.

What made the difference? Through years of study, I discovered that a constant flow of thoughts in the background of my mind was affecting everything in my life: how I related to others, my physical well being, my decision making, and my overall attitude. When I understood how the mind operates and developed a way to work with it, I was able to create my own moments of peace.

The mind is always busy generating thoughts, whether you are aware of them or not. The thoughts can be simple and neutral—observations and comments about what's happening at the moment; or they can be judgmental, negative, and harmful, as when they tell you how worthless you are or how hopeless your life is. We can call this constant stream of thoughts "mental chatter."

Negative mental chatter is the cause of a problematic life. Often the ongoing thoughts are preoccupied with something regrettable from the past— an event that happened earlier in your life or last week or today. Or the thoughts may be worries about the future—things that may or may not happen tomorrow or in a few years. As your mind goes over and over these thoughts, they become distorted and exaggerated. They inflate into stories or dramas you hear time and again as the mind repeats them. Since you don't know they are only stories, you believe them. And the more convinced you are that they are true, the more you are influenced by them, and the more you experience stress and depression.

Think about a story a friend has told you or you have heard on the news. The more often you hear it, the more likely you are to believe it. The same thing happens when your mind repeatedly tells you that you are unlovable, or you always do things wrong, or there's trouble ahead. Eventually you believe it's true.

Negative mental chatter plays a large role in keeping you from enjoying your life. It is painful to listen to the mind's critical input, and you might respond out loud (such as in a burst of anger), or you might keep your reaction to yourself and remain silent. Either way, if you believe your mind's criticism, you suffer. Not only do you feel the pain inside, those around you sense your drama and are affected by it.

Introduction

In this book, I will teach you a variety of easy methods to interrupt the mind's dialogue. The more often you elect to step out of your stream of negative thoughts, the less influence they will have on your feelings and moods. This is especially important if you suffer from stress, moodiness, or depression. As you turn down the volume of mental chatter, life will become easier.

Using this method is a process. It will take time. If you are expecting a quick fix, you are likely to become frustrated. But when you begin to experience moments of peace and glimpses of clarity, you may want to continue this process for the rest of your life.

The chatter in your head has always been there, and it will not turn off by the time you finish this book. But by following my plan, you can start turning down the volume. How far you go depends on the amount of effort you put into it.

I hope my journey will help you find your own way to peace.

Chapter 2
My Story

I often felt a sense of guilt because I was not living the life I had been taught I was supposed to live—a life without sin.

Chapter 2

My Story

When I was a boy, the central theme in my house was religion. My parents' strict religious beliefs became confining walls for me. From an early age, I listened to our minister preach Hellfire and damnation three or four times a week. Hearing these messages from the cradle on, I took them literally. My concept of God was a mean and unforgiving entity, and I lived my days in fear that if I didn't walk the straight and narrow, I would burn in a fiery Hell when I died.

When I reached high school, I bought my first car, a 1949 Plymouth. Now I was able to get around, and my

Chapter 2

world expanded. The rules in my house still existed, and I still had my fears, but I felt less confined. I discovered there was a great big world out there, and not everyone was guided by the religion my family practiced—at least, not most of my friends. I hid that side of my life from them.

For the first time, I felt part of a group, part of something that wasn't steered by moral guidelines and my fear of retribution if I broke the rules. I tried hard to be one of the guys. My friends and I concentrated on sports, and when we weren't playing or watching some game, we turned our focus to just plain teenage fun.

My Story

Still, I often felt a sense of guilt because I was not living the life I had been taught I was supposed to live—a life without sin. I was not a criminal, just a "worldly" person like all my friends, but deep inside, I feared I was doomed. I believed that being a worldly person meant Hell and damnation for me.

Not long after my high school days, at age 20, I married. It was a time of great change. Within three years, my wife and I had two children. I was now a husband and father, working at a steady warehouse job. Since my first automobile purchase in high school, I had always loved cars, so when an opportunity arose at a Ford

Chapter 2

dealership in Des Moines, Iowa, I took it. In a short time I realized I had found my niche: I was pretty handy at peddling cars.

Three years later, I was promoted to the sales manager position. I was young to be directing a staff of salespeople two or three times my age, but they accepted me as their "coach," and together we produced high volume sales. I was working nearly 70 hours a week, hustling in and out of my office each day.

As I hurried back and forth, I could see into the owner's office, which was right next to mine and three times the size. He always left his door open and propped his feet up on his spotless desk. I said to myself, "That's the job I want."

So, at the age of 31, with the help of my father-in-law, my banker, and the Ford Motor Company, I went into business for myself. I purchased a Ford-Lincoln-Mercury dealership in the wonderful community of Carroll, Iowa, 90 miles northwest of Des Moines.

It was a tall task running this kind of business at such a young age. However, I populated my dealership with a team of great people, and car sales grew.

A successful and growing business doesn't necessarily mean the owner is living a life of ease.

Chapter 2

Even with all my drive to get ahead, I was developing a pattern of increasing moodiness. Because the pattern was developing so gradually, I did not identify this growing tendency in myself.

Chapter 3
Looking for a Way Out

I found I could actually identify and do something about the negative feelings that were my constant companions. I was fascinated with the possibility of changing my life.

Chapter 3

Looking for a Way Out

In 1985, I was 40 years old. Arguments at home were becoming more frequent. It seemed as if my wife and I had one good-sized spat each month. We went for marriage counseling.

After we each filled out a questionnaire (which was actually a test to identify depression) and handed them in, the psychologist looked at me and said, "Roland, you are what we consider severely depressed." The doctor decided right then and there to devote our weekly sessions primarily to healing me, as opposed to training us in the communications techniques traditionally taught to couples in distress.

After a few visits, the psychologist suggested I meet with her associate, a psychiatrist, to get a prescription for meds. It was my introduction to Prozac and the onset of 18 long years of taking psychiatric drugs. But more importantly, with this doctor I experienced an epiphany: He told me that, in his opinion, many religious tenets are decided by man—that man, not God, had made up the rules of my religion.

What a concept! Because many of my dark thoughts came from my deeply religious upbringing, this idea was transforming. If that was the case—if the rules had been made by man, and all men are fallible—maybe what I had been taught wasn't true, and I could, after all, shed the restrictions of my religious beliefs. With this revelation, the fear that had been imprisoning me slowly began to dissolve.

The psychologist also recommended a book about how emotions affect our perceptions. Little did she know that I had never read a book in my life. I couldn't concentrate. Getting through high school had been a challenge—my grades had been pitiful. But I bought the book, took it home, and found I could hardly put it down. The author suggested I could actually identify and do something about the negative feelings that were my constant companions. I was fascinated with the possibility of changing my life.

The book was my first exposure to cognitive therapy, which is based on the concept that our emotions distort our perception of reality. It offered techniques to identify such distorted perceptions. It taught me how to put my negative thoughts on paper, determine if my statements were irrational, and if they were, to follow up with rational responses. For example, I wrote down, "I never do anything right." By putting it down on paper, I could see I was using all-or-nothing thinking. Obviously, I do a lot of things right. So I wrote that down: "I do a lot of things right." By practicing this exercise, I found I could actually break myself out of a bad mood. What a discovery! I made it part of my daily routine, and depending on how I was feeling, I would use it two or three times a day. It always helped.

One day after using the technique and feeling really good, I suddenly thought, "So, if I can break free of a bad mood by using this exercise, why do I need meds?"

Chapter 3

Years later, I came to realize how powerful that particular question was. It stayed with me throughout the many years of my search for happiness.

Chapter 4
Crisis

I had decided the cleanest and most convenient way to end it all was to gas myself with the fumes from my car.

Chapter 4

Crisis

Although I was taking a variety of medications and the writing technique was giving me relief for short periods of time, my depression was still debilitating. I was desperately seeking a way out. Luckily, as owner of my car business, I was able to delegate most of the work, which gave me time to search for answers that would allow me to free myself from depression.

From the outside, no one would have been able to see how I was struggling. I was very good at putting on a front. I looked like I had it together: I was a successful

Chapter 4

businessman; I had been elected chairman of a state-wide industry organization. I had a new house in the fanciest part of town. I also owned a winter home in Scottsdale, Arizona. In other words, I was at the pinnacle of my material world.

But on the inside, I struggled every day to overcome mountains of stress. I had overextended myself financially in order to create the image I thought would bring me happiness. I dreamed of building an empire of automobile dealerships, and I started yet another business across town. In order to maintain all this, I needed to continue making lots of money.

Crisis

In 1997, my 32-year marriage fell apart. The divorce was very difficult. I am convinced my depression was a factor leading to our distress. When one partner is depressed, the language of the relationship is divided: the depressed partner often has an emotional perspective, while the other partner is likely to maintain a more rational outlook. But no matter the cause, my divorce was painful, and it took me a long time to heal. I haunted the self-help sections of book stores. I tried to distract myself in any way I could, but although I kept myself busy with activities, my life felt hollow.

Chapter 4

At a high-school class reunion the following year, I ran into an old friend. She lived near Kansas City, Missouri, and didn't always attend the reunions, so I hadn't seen her in a long time. We had a great conversation that night, and we started dating two weeks later.

For two and a half years, we enjoyed a long distance relationship. I was still fighting depression, but she seemed to understand and put up with my moods. In December 2000, we married, and my bride moved from Kansas City to Carroll.

Crisis

Three months later, my new wife decided to take an out-of-town trip to spend time with her mother and niece. On a cold, wintry morning, she left the house before I did.

I was aware that it was one of my difficult days. The more I thought about the issues in my life, the lower I felt. I hung around the house a while, trying to deal with my pitch-black thoughts. Typically, at this time of morning I would head to my dealership. But as I left the house, I realized I just wasn't ready to face anyone at the store. I've always believed employees take an attitude signal from their boss, so I made a habit of projecting a positive appearance. But on this day, I didn't have the strength to maintain the façade. Even though the day was bright white from the snow, my vision was getting darker by the minute. I stopped at the McDonald's drive-up window for a cup of coffee and then drove aimlessly for what seemed like a long, long time.

I couldn't find an ounce of hope about anything in my life. My divorce was still unsettling for me; my new marriage was feeling complicated. Financial issues were weighing heavily on me.

I suddenly concluded there was only one way out.

Crisis

Over the years, when I had experienced periods of low outlook, I had considered the idea of suicide. I now decided the cleanest and most convenient way was to gas myself with the fumes from my car. In this state of mind, there was no rationality, no thought of loved ones; actually, I wasn't thinking of anybody but myself.

My first thought was to find a garage. After mulling over various possibilities, I determined the only way to get this done privately was to pull into my own garage at home. I drove there, hit the garage door opener, and pulled in. I pushed the button to close the door behind me, and I left the car running.

I rolled down my driver's side window a couple inches to let in the fumes. After the motor had run for ten minutes or so, nothing had happened. I wasn't feeling dizzy. I stared at the steering wheel, trying to make sense of my passing thoughts. I rolled the window down more, and then even more. Still, the fumes were not getting to me. I spent a long time just sitting there, the motor running, passing the time.

Crisis

Occasionally I glanced at the clock. I had pulled into the garage at noon, and it was now 12:45. I suddenly realized I should write out a will and leave it next to me for someone to find. My wife and I had recently updated our wills with our attorney, but with all the legal language, they seemed too complicated. I just wanted to make it clear and easy. I pulled a legal pad out of my briefcase and very neatly wrote out my wishes as simply and clearly as I could. Of course, I never put any thought into how horrific this was going to be for my unsuspecting wife when she came home and found me dead.

In some ways, time was going by really fast, and in other ways, time was dragging, passing very slowly. It was now 1:30, and I was still alive.

I left the car running and stepped out. By now a smoky fog had accumulated throughout the garage. I walked back to the tail pipe. I thought it might work better if I could get my head down near the exhaust and breathe in.

I didn't want to get my pants dirty, so I went to the front of the garage and got a towel. I put it down next to the tail pipe and got on my knees. I leaned over and slowly inhaled.

I was feeling a little dazed, but just ever so slightly.

Finally, I got up and held the towel close to the tailpipe, trying to soak up all the fumes. I brought it to my face, inhaling and sucking in. Then I got back into the car. I looked at the clock. It showed 1:45. An hour and forty-five minutes had passed.

With a foggy head, I remembered I had a haircut appointment at 2:00 p.m. What if I didn't show up? The barber would call the dealership, the office employees would start looking for me, and I wouldn't be dead. People would know I'd tried to kill myself, and my reputation as a respected businessman would be shattered.

Chapter 4

Suddenly, it became very important to keep that appointment.

I turned off the engine and hit the garage door button. It was a windy day, and a strong gust immediately whisked away the fog, clearing the garage. I tore up the will, rolled down all the windows, and drove to the barbershop. I walked in to see my friend the barber, right on time.

Everything was back to normal.

I was still alive.

Coming to such a low point in my life, into that dark place, and then coming out of it again gave me a new

appreciation for just being alive. The depression had
not gone away. But I suddenly realized that this life was
worth fighting for, particularly a life free of depression.
So with new energy, I started a more vigorous search for
a way into the light.

Chapter 5
Moving On

I spent thousands of hours reading everything I could get my hands on about depression. I was **determined** to find the way out.

Chapter 5

Moving On

By this time the dealership was beginning to show signs of my neglect, so I decided to sell it while I still could. When the sale was complete, for all intents and purposes, I was retired. My wife and I pulled up stakes and moved to Kansas City. In my new home, I found a renowned psychiatrist to take over the management of my daily anti-depressant meds and talk-therapy sessions.

Life was challenging. I was in a new city, with all the accompanying uncertainties. I had been used to my routines, and now I had to learn everything from scratch: what was available, where things were located, how to get what I needed. A new marriage at fifty brings its own set of difficulties. I was still dealing with my divorce, and my relationship with my kids was strained. The sale of the business had not gone as easily as I had hoped, so there were financial pressures. My depression continued.

The cognitive therapy writing exercise was still my only coping tool. It could usually free me from moodiness for short periods—sometimes an hour or maybe a few hours. At the very least, I was able to detect when an emotional mood was coming on. I was able to sit down and fairly quickly resolve the problem, feel better, and go on from there. I felt lucky to have something that worked, even if it provided only temporary relief. I knew millions of other people were having emotional problems like mine, but very few of them had this particular magic trick at their disposal.

Over the previous 18 years, I had spent thousands of hours reading everything I could get my hands on about depression. Retired, I now had more time to do my research. In one summer alone, I read or skimmed almost

Chapter 5

300 books, trying to pinpoint as many opinions about depression as I could find. I concentrated on new books, searching for the latest theories. I was determined to find the way out.

Chapter 6
My Breakthrough and POPs

I determined to live more of my life in the **present**, *not in the chaos of the past or the future, where I had been living for so many years.*

Chapter 6

My Breakthrough and POPs

One day in February of 2003, after years of studying about depression, I came home and said to my wife, "Honey, I feel like I'm about to think my way out of depression."

On a morning two weeks later, I woke up, sat straight up, and looked around. I had never before experienced such clarity. My vision was crystal clear. My senses were keen. I couldn't believe what I was experiencing. The depression was gone for the first time in decades.

Chapter 6

My wife was downstairs fixing breakfast. I couldn't wait to share this with her. I tiptoed to the bottom of the stairs and peeked around the corner. I didn't have to say a word. She saw the look on my face, ran over to me, and gave me a big hug. We've been celebrating ever since. It was a moment I'll never forget, because from then on, my life has not been the same.

When I saw my psychiatrist a few weeks later at a regularly scheduled session, he was shocked to see how different I looked. I told him the story. He was perplexed—I think he thought I was having a manic experience—and wanted to start seeing me every two weeks rather than monthly. After a few sessions, he became convinced the shift was real. He said, "You're a walking miracle."

I had no idea what exactly had happened—if something had caused this breakthrough, or if there was simply no explanation for it. It truly *did* feel like a miracle.

I discontinued talk therapy, and under my doctor's careful supervision, weaned myself off the medications. My search was over.

Many things were changing in my life. I was feeling much better. My energy increased considerably. Every day I was gaining clarity in my mind, which meant I could think more sharply and had less need for sleep. I was continually amazed to hear the birds singing and see the beautiful sky.

From a social standpoint, the effects were immediate. My self-confidence perked up, and relationships started growing. I was able to better communicate with others. My family and close friends witnessed a dynamic change in my overall demeanor, including even a change in my voice.

I was pretty much free of moodiness for an entire year—the longest I had ever experienced life without moods. But over time, the darkness began to creep back in, and I was sure if I didn't do something to maintain my equilibrium, I would slip back into depression. I was determined not to let that happen. I went back to my studies.

Many authors talked about the thought stream in the mind. Many others discussed the benefits of getting into the present moment. I was fascinated. It seemed to me those two concepts held the key to my freedom.

I began to understand what caused my moods. I realized that all my life, I was constantly thinking about one problem after another. I was a prisoner of my mind, which was always engaged in a story from the past or a fantasy about the future. I realized the anger and fear I had constantly felt was a result of my mind generating unhappy scenarios from the past or scary possibilities about the future and then exaggerating them into ongoing dramas. Those thoughts affected my feelings and actions. They caused sadness, depression, anxiety, withdrawal, and fits of anger. I began to recognize the enormity of my mind occupation. I realized I had been suffering from over-thinking, a victim of my own busy mind.

The idea of keeping your thoughts in present time, not focusing on the past or the future, showed up in many of the sources I explored. This fit with what I was learning about the thought stream. Since all my drama was about the past and the future, it made sense to try to keep my thoughts from dwelling there. I became convinced that peace and serenity could exist only in the present time, when I was not thinking about the past or the future.

I determined to live more of my life in the present, not in the chaos of the past or the future, where I had been living for so many years. If I could increase the time I spent in the present and decrease the time I spent thinking about the past or the future, I would be taking a step in the right direction.

Chapter 6

These two ideas—the thought stream and being in the present moment—changed everything. I knew what I needed: a way to interrupt my mind when it was spinning dramatic stories and get me momentarily into the present. If I could find a way to break into my thoughts, I could cut off the stories before I was swamped by the emotions they evoked.

And from there, Pieces of Peace—self-generated moments of clarity—emerged. I developed exercises that would enable me to maintain the freedom I had found. Before I talk about POPs, though, let me give you some background about the thought stream.

Chapter 7
Dwelling in Thoughts

Whether you are dwelling in the past or the future, the turbulence from the mental chatter is a self-inflicted torture.

Chapter 7

Dwelling in Thoughts

Most of us develop a tendency to dwell in thought, and because we live in time, our thoughts can be about the past, the future, or the present. When the mind conjures up recollections of the past, there is likely to be distortion or a misremembering of what happened. There is also likely to be magnification of anger, hurt, guilt, or other emotions. When the mind considers the future, the distortion can come in the form of scenarios that may or may not happen, but it can create anxiety, fear, and stress.

Chapter 7

In either case, the more time we spend thinking about the past or future, the more warped the picture becomes. The danger is that during our daily functioning, our thoughts are often—perhaps even mostly—in the past or the future. Not only are we lost in a fantasy about the past or the future—which is likely to be making us miserable—we are missing out on experiencing the life that is happening right now, in the present.

When you think about the past, there are many ways to make yourself unhappy. You can think about how badly someone treated you and get lost in self-pity or revenge fantasies; you can think about something you did that you wish you hadn't and get lost in regret. You can think about a missed opportunity and become mired in what might have been. All of these thoughts can become exaggerated to the point they keep you from experiencing happiness in the present. Not only do you convince yourself of the truth of the distorted scenarios, you may even try to convince others about your story, thereby gaining their support, increasing the drama, and reinforcing your misery.

When you think of something in the future, it is guaranteed to be inaccurate. Why? Because it hasn't yet happened, and it is not real. When you are forecasting a situation, you are out of focus, so to speak. The more time you spend ruminating about the future, the more magnified and distorted the picture gets. The drama becomes so alluring and powerful, you think what you're imagining is real. Your mind does this so often that you develop a habit of creating distorted thinking.

Whether you are dwelling in the past or the future, the turbulence from the mental chatter is a self-inflicted torture.

Dwelling in Thoughts

A tendency to ruminate in thought accelerates through different stages of life. Envision a group of toddlers during their typical day. Do you see them spending much time lost in thought? No, not at all. They are usually completely in the moment; their reality is what is happening right now.

Now picture a group of twenty-something folks. Imagine their typical behaviors. They might spend a little more time in thought.

How much mental contemplation do you visualize a group of forty- to fifty-year-olds doing? By this stage of life, they probably are quite often lost in thought.

Lastly, consider a typical group of elderly people. How much mental processing might you observe in them? Probably quite a bit.

As life progresses, people experience mishaps, surprises, hurdles, disappointments, and tragedies. This, of course, provides opportunity for living in the past, thinking about what happened and what we wish had happened. As you get older, you typically experience a subtle increase in unfocused thought, each minute, each hour, each day, each week, each month, and each year.

Dwelling in Thoughts

Let me distinguish between using the mind to figure out a problem and letting the mind wander where it will, lingering in the past and the future. Obviously, you need to use your mind to get through the day—to accomplish activities, to complete tasks at home and at work, to deal with the complications of everyday life.

When I talk about "dwelling in thought," I'm referring to those periods when you are not conscious of your mind working: "the lights are on, but nobody's home." You have probably had the experience of driving on the highway and passing the exit you intended to take. It's quite likely you missed it because your mind was humming along without your conscious awareness, and only when you passed the exit sign did you suddenly "come back to yourself." I experienced this often when performing a routine function. For example, when I'd brush my teeth or sit at a stoplight in the car, or even when I drove down the road, I wasn't aware of what I was doing physically, but was actually lost in thought.

I use the term "spans of unawareness" to refer to the times when we allow our thoughts to spin out—spin stories—without our noticing. At those times, we lose track of reality. Our mental chatter takes us out of the moment. The longer the span of unawareness, the more distortion builds and the more deeply we live in our unwanted emotions. When this happens on a minute-to-minute and hour-to-hour basis, it can develop into a life of moodiness.

The real danger comes from a lack of understanding about the mind's tendency to create stories. Most people don't know they are being continually misguided, and as a result, they make poor decisions, often from an emotional standpoint. Many times, they pay the price for making decisions based on emotions in their relationships, finances, business, health, or other areas.

Chapter 7

Let's do an exercise to see how unruly the mind is…
how much it does not want to stay in the present.

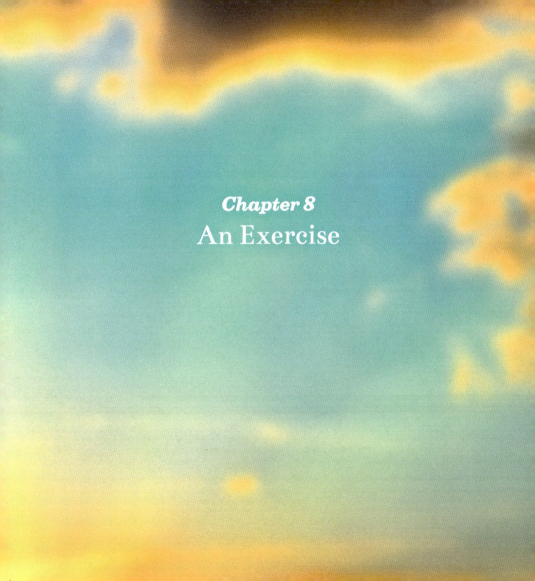

Chapter 8

An Exercise

First, recognize you are not captive to the mind. The mind is not your master. Until now, you have unknowingly allowed the mind's activity to lead you.

Chapter 8

An Exercise

The mind is constantly producing a stream of thoughts about all kinds of things. These thoughts often relate to events that have happened in the past or might happen in the future. Very seldom does the mind fix on what is happening in the present moment. You can see this for yourself and actually watch your mind doing its dance by performing the following exercise.

1. Find a clock or a watch with a second hand
   (not a digital clock or watch).
2. Put the clock or watch in front of you. For the
   next 60 seconds, you are going to be observing
   your thoughts.

An Exercise

3. During this time, watch your thoughts while they're streaming. If you pay close attention, you will notice you're thinking about what you're going to do next, what you might have for dinner, or how you feel about the argument you had with your co-worker yesterday. If you notice these kinds of thoughts, you are not in the present. You are in the past or the future.

4. When the 60 seconds are over, estimate how many actual seconds you were focused in present time rather than in the past or the future. Be honest

with yourself about this estimate. No one but you

will know your answer.

> When I did this exercise, I was astonished
> to realize how actively my thoughts were
> streaming. Thoughts were passing by so
> quickly, there was just no way to keep track!
> I had to estimate the time I had spent in the
> present. I estimated I was in the present for
> only 2 seconds out of that minute.

5. Write down the number of seconds you were in the

    present. (If you find yourself in the same situation

    that I did and you can't give an accurate number,

    then write down an estimate.) _____.

An Exercise

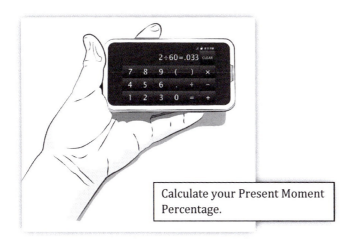

Calculate your Present Moment Percentage.

6. Next, use a calculator to determine what percentage
   of time during the 60-second period your thoughts
   were in the present moment. (We will use this
   number later as you learn how to increase the time
   you spend in the present.) To do this, divide your

number—even if it's an estimate—by 60 to get a percentage. For example, I was in the present for 2 seconds, so the calculation was 2.0 ÷ 60.0 = .033 (3%). This meant that for 97% of that sampling, my mind was occupied in the past or in the future!

7. **Write down your Present Moment Percentage:**

_____.

This exercise should give you an idea of just how busy your mind is. This was only a 60-second test, and you were trying your best to be present. You could barely keep track of what you were thinking, right? Just imagine what your runaway mind is doing throughout the day.

An Exercise

Staying in the Present

How do you know if you're in the present? You are in the present when you are focusing on something at hand: the feeling of the chair beneath you; the sound of the clock ticking; the sight of the sunlight coming through the window; the warmth of your face or the cool air around you.

What Now?

So now you've learned the cause of your stress and your moodiness: They are caused by the stories your mind makes up about the past or the future. And you are beginning to understand that you have had little awareness of your mind's activity.

If you are tired of the struggle and want to go in a new direction—if you have exhausted yourself with worry, fear, and anger—if you no longer want to live a life filled with roller-coaster emotions—you can do something about it.

First, recognize you are not captive to the mind. The mind is not your master. Until now, you have unknowingly allowed the mind's activity to lead you. You didn't plan to create those negative thoughts. But if you listened to them and believed them, you allowed them to make you feel bad. ***I am going to teach you how to become aware of the ongoing mental stream and how to interrupt its flow.*** If you break off the mental chatter that's sending you on downward spirals—even briefly—you will experience refreshing moments in the present.

However, it's not likely you are going to wake up one morning with the mind's negative dialogue simply gone. It doesn't work that way. But you can very easily start, one step at a time, to reduce the disturbing noise of the mind.

In doing so, you will learn how to lessen your suffering, shed some of your painful experiences, dilute the magnitude of your debilitating moods, and weaken the stranglehold these negative and excessive thoughts have on you. The process will be gradual. Have patience.

Chapter 9
Pieces of Peace (POPs)

You don't have to believe everything the mind tells you.

Chapter 9

Pieces of Peace
(POPs)

By doing the clock exercise, you discovered just how little time you spend in the present—and how much of the time you are lost in thought. Now, where do you go from here? How do you change? What worked for me was Pieces of Peace—POPs.

A Piece of Peace is an intentional momentary breakup of the constant thought stream. During the moment of a POP, you are in peace. For one brief moment, you have broken up your span of unawareness, and your agonizing mind has stopped its busy chatter.

Chapter 9

You are going to learn how to create these awareness-moments. You will create a new habit of observing the mind's over-thinking and interrupting it before it gets too intense.

As a rule, the longer the mind is running in a span of unawareness, the more intense the internal drama gets; your thoughts become more magnified and distorted, causing more pain and suffering. If your present average span of unawareness or mental stream is two minutes, then occasional, intentional POPs can begin to shorten its length and intensity. If, for instance, you think about some dreadful possibility in the future for only one minute—versus two minutes—you will suffer much less anxiety. It's like reducing mountains down to speed bumps. Once you experiment with creating POPs, you will come to realize you are in charge and you do not have to be a victim of your busy mind. You can be the driver of your life and create space for happiness.

Perform a POP Exercise

Stop for a second, right now. Take hold of this page in this book. Hold the edge of it apart from the next page. Now, take the next page and separate it from this page. Hold the two pages separate, but next to each other. Examine and compare the thickness of the two pages. Determine if one is thicker than the other.

———◦◦◦———

During that few seconds, you were in present time. You were not thinking about the past or the future. That very brief moment was a "Piece of Peace," or a POP. You were not "in depression" or "under stress" during that moment. Were you?

No, you weren't. This demonstrates that depression and stress are not "conditions" that have a grip on you.

You had a choice at that moment to take control, and in doing so, you alleviated your pain momentarily.

Now, if you immediately thought, "Yes, but my problems are still there and they didn't go away," there you go! That's what the mind will say. You can latch onto that thought and take it as far as you want and head into more misery. Or you can recognize it for the thought that it is and watch it fade away.

The more you believe what the mind says, the larger the problem becomes. You don't have to believe everything the mind tells you.

There Are Many Ways to Create a POP

Concentrate for two or three seconds on any of the following.

- Envision your heart inside your body at this very moment. Imagine it as a red, vibrant organ, its valves opening and closing in the aliveness of its operation.

- Envision your lungs working inside your body. As you breathe in and out, picture your lungs inflating and deflating.

- Stop and look at a tree. Admire its shape and beauty. Observe a flower or the blue sky or listen to a bird's song—anything that pleases your eyes or ears. Nature is an excellent source of POPs.

- Watch a dog or a cat. This can be a refreshing way to temporarily break free of thoughts. Just gaze into their eyes or note their subtle movements.

- If you're inside, look around the room and observe its spaciousness, not the furnishings. If you are outdoors, sense the air around you. Breathe it in.

- Observe a tiny spot on your shirt, your hand, or your desk. Focus on it for a couple seconds.

- Make and hold direct eye contact with another person.

- Listen to any and all sounds around you.

- Smell aromas in your presence.

- Feel different textures for a brief moment.

You can develop your own tricks to interrupt your mental stream. I encourage you to create POPs and do them as often as you can. As you do, you will acquire an increasing awareness of your mind's unrelenting noise. And the more you become aware of the noise, the more you will be motivated to practice Pieces of Peace. The more times each day you create a POP, the stronger the new habit will become. Eventually, interrupting your stream of thoughts will not seem like an exercise; it will become an instinct.

In the course of time, you will develop an automatic awareness of the mind's activity. The more often you interrupt the mindstream, the more time you will spend in the present moment. And the more you interrupt your thoughts, the less power your runaway mind will have on your outlook.

Chapter 10
Tracking Your Progress

I could see I was making progress, even if it was in small increments—staying present for a greater percentage of the time.

Chapter 10

Tracking Your Progress

Whenever you start thinking about making a big change in your life, it's easy to get excited and think, "Oh, I want to do this every day!" But then at some point, it seems too burdensome, and you stop. And the excitement and possibility for change dies. How can you keep the excitement alive? In my journey, tracking my progress was the key to maintaining my enthusiasm.

What follows is an option you can use to help you achieve success. Not everybody needs a log or journal as a motivator. If you do the POPs and begin to feel a change in your life, and you don't need or want to keep track of your "progress" day to day, that's fine. I enjoy documenting my activities, so for me it was fun. Keeping track supported my new routine and motivated me to keep going.

I kept a record based on my "golf ball theory." Golf has always been one of my passions. I love the game. It took me years to realize why I used to play so often: concentrating on the game allowed me to escape my constant worrying.

If the ball I was playing got scuffed up or cut, I'd throw it into the bag and take out a new one. And whenever I'd find a lost ball in the rough, I'd throw it into my bag. Eventually I accumulated a sizable collection of undesirable balls. Although I normally rode a cart, I still had to lug my bag at times. Every now and then, when I lifted up my bag, it would feel so heavy that I would stop to take inventory. Sure enough, each time the culprit was excess golf balls. When I finally got rid of them, how much lighter the bag was!

Years ago I found I was gradually gaining weight. I hated the idea of having to buy all new trousers. One day I looked up "weight of a golf ball" on the Internet. A golf ball weighs 1.6 ounces, exactly one-tenth of a pound (16 ounces). I thought about my past failures at weight loss. Whenever I'd set a goal to lose weight and stepped on the scale, I'd get discouraged. One time my weight would be down one pound, and another time up two pounds, and so forth. Suddenly I realized if I could lose just one "golf ball" of weight at a time and be able to document it, it might motivate me to keep going. I needed to measure my progress by tenths of a pound. Small steps, but very doable.

I also realized if I based my progress not on my last weigh-in, but on the trend of my weight, I would no longer count every "up" day as a failure, and I could be encouraged by my incremental downward progress. I created a chart for my weigh-ins. I recorded my weight every few days and then added up my accumulated weight and divided it by the number of entries. The important number to me was my average weight. Was it trending up or down? It was usually down (see Figure 1).

Sure enough, it started to work. It was easy to stay motivated. It was simply a matter of changing my attitude. When I looked at my average column and saw I had lost another tenth of a pound, it was like taking a golf ball out of my pocket and no longer hauling it around. By concentrating on tiny steps—one golf ball at

Cumulative Weight ÷ Number of Entries = Average Weight

Example: 386 ÷ 2 = 193.0

A	B	C	D
Entry	Daily Weight	Cumulative Weight	Average Weight
1	194	194	**194.0**
2	192	386	**193.0**
3	193	579	**193.0**
4	192	771	**192.8**
↓	↓	↓	↓
42	187	7901	**188.1**
43	184	8085	**188.0**
44	184	8269	**187.9**
45	183	8452	**187.8**

One-tenth of a pound is the weight of a golf ball.

Figure 1: Golf Ball Weight Trend Chart

a time—it was easier to lose weight consistently. When I had lost a full pound in my average column, I had eliminated 10 golf balls.

The only diet changes were mental. If I had a plate of food in front of me, I might leave a couple of bites on the plate, or I might choose not to have dessert occasionally so I could eliminate one more golf ball.

This process was so successful that my weight dropped from the 190s to the 170s. I stayed in my same-sized trousers and benefited in many other ways. I was finally able to lose weight because for the first time ever, I stayed motivated. I was concentrating on one thing only—my next small step.

How Does the Golf Ball Theory Relate to Mind Awareness?

When I became convinced that the absolute answer to happiness, fulfillment, and peace was less past and future mind occupation, I realized I could track on paper how long I was staying in the present, just as I did when I tracked my weight loss. When I could see in black and white that I was making progress—staying present for a greater percentage of the time, even if it was in very small increments—I would be motivated to continue. It would be my own personal present moment "batting average."

The chart I developed had five columns, as shown in Figure 2. In the back of the book are copies of the same chart, called *Daily Log*. You can make your own copies to help you track your progress.

The first entry on the chart is the information from the clock exercise you did for one minute. (By the way...you don't need to do the clock exercise again. Its purpose was to demonstrate how active your mind is, and to create your starting point.) Enter 1 in Column A and the date you did the exercise in Column B. Then write your "Present Moment Percentage" (the number you calculated in Chapter 8) in Column C. Because this is your first entry, write the same number in Columns D and E.

Daily Log of % Time Spent in the Present

A	B	C	D	E
Entry	Date	% Time in Present Today	Total of Entries from Column C	Average % Time in Present (Present Moment Percentage)
1	3-09	③	3	3.0

Figure 2: First Entry in Daily Log

At this point, you are doing your POPs frequently and stopping your mental chatter for brief moments throughout the day. Now you will fill in the chart, line by line, by estimating the percentage of time you spent in the present for the entire day. At the end of the day, ask yourself, "What percentage of time do I estimate I spent in present time today?" The answer might be, "Well, it was a good day…I've done a lot of POPs…I'd say today was about 4%."

Enter your daily number as follows. In Column A, write the entry number (see Figure 3). After entering the date in Column B, enter the day's percentage in Column C (shown as 4 in the figure) and add the two numbers in the column together. Put the total (shown

Daily Log of % Time Spent in the Present
(*Example:* 7 ÷ 2 = 3.5)

A	B	C	D	E
Entry	Date	% Time in Present Today	Total of Entries from Column C	Average % Time in Present (Present Moment Percentage)
1	3-09	3	3	3.0
2	3-11	4	7	3.5

Figure 3: Second Entry in Daily Log

as 7 in the figure) in Column D. To find the average percentage of time spent in the present, divide the number in Column D (7) by the number in Column A (2) and put the resulting number in Column E (3.5).

This is your Average Present Moment Percentage. It is important to use the decimal point to a tenth of a percent. Just as when I was measuring my weight loss in golf-ball-size increments, you are measuring your progress by small gains.

Each time you make an entry, fill in a new row and use the new figures in your calculations. As you continue your practice and fill in additional rows, you will be able to see a trend in the E Column (Present Moment Percentage) that shows you are spending a larger percentage of time in the present. Similar to the way a batting average works, not all days are stellar; but if you focus on

Daily Log of % Time Spent in the Present

A	B	C	D	E
Entry	Date	% Time in Present Today	Total of Entries from Column C	Average % Time in Present (Present Moment Percentage)
1	3-09	3	3	3.0
2	3-11	4	7	3.5
3	3-12	5	12	4.0
4	3-16	4	16	4.0
5	3-17	7	23	4.6

Figure 4: Watching the Upward Trend of Your Present Moment Percentage

the trend and not each day's number, you are likely to
see a gradual positive movement.

Tips for Using the Daily Log

- The math may seem complicated at first, but after you do it a couple times, it will be easy.

- I encourage you to continue logging an entry every day or at least every few days to keep track of your progress. If you forget to log in, don't try to estimate your number for yesterday. Your recall by then won't be as accurate. Just log in at the end of today. These calculations are based on trends, which are determined by the number of chronological entries.

- It's important to recognize that setting a new direction is much easier if you can measure your success with documentation and gain reinforcement by observing the progress of your new direction. If you get discouraged, look back at where you started.

- To stay motivated, don't set goals. Just decide you are taking one small step at a time in the right direction toward less mental distortion. And in just a matter of days, you will likely sense glimpses of peace. It may be as subtle as hearing a bird sing or noticing something in your everyday surroundings that you had never observed before.

By moving the number in the Present Moment Percentage column one tenth of a percent at a time in an upward direction, you will see progress. Every small bit of time directed toward peace reduces the number of unconscious thoughts that lead to stress and depression. As the percentage rises, it will start tipping the scale toward well being in your life ahead.

In the first few weeks I used the chart, I raised my average time in the present from 3% to 10%—a 356% improvement. And it became easier and easier each time. Using the chart helped me maintain my enthusiasm for the process.

Daily Log of % Time Spent in the Present

A	B	C	D	E
Entry	Date	% Time in Present Today	Total of Entries from Column C	Average % Time in Present (Present Moment Percentage)
1	3-09	3	3	3.0
2	3-11	4	7	3.5
3	3-12	5	12	4.0
4	3-16	4	16	4.0
5	3-17	7	23	4.6
↓	↓	↓	↓	↓
14	4-10	9	90	6.4
15	4-13	12	102	6.8
16	4-16	11	113	7.1
17	4-19	13	126	7.4
↓	↓	↓	↓	↓
25	5-18	18	245	9.8
26	5-21	16	261	10.0
27	5-24	19	280	10.4
28	5-28	20	300	(10.7)

356% Improvement! ↗
More Peace!

Figure 5: Persistent Practice Provides More Peace

Tracking Your Progress

It's quite common these days to hear someone say, "To find peace, just live in present time." And it's true. Peace lies in the present moment. If you are temporarily void of your mind's negative noise, you become temporarily peaceful. But to actually get to that peace, you must create the habit of observing the mind by doing the practice.

Don't lose heart. It may not be possible to live in peace every moment, but experiencing an increased sense of peace and serenity is possible. As you learn the simple act of directing your thinking, you will simultaneously reduce your habit of being stressed and depressed. With practice, it will work for you.

Chapter 11
Encouragement

Once you feel it the first time, you will want more. And then you will be on your way to recovery.

Chapter 11

Encouragement

When I started playing golf, I was conscious of all the technical aspects of the swing. As time went on, I began to enjoy the game more and more, because I became less conscious of the swing itself, which by then had become automatic to me. This is the result and benefit of practice.

For me, mind awareness was much easier to learn than golf. My mind was always with me, so I could practice as often as I wished, and soon the habit of going to present time became automatic. The benefits were remarkable, so naturally I wanted to keep doing it.

In your early stages, you will find yourself following your lifetime habit of past and future mind occupation with its powerful force of drama and negativity. You are simply following the trail that many have traveled before. You created a tendency to listen to and believe the mind, and you are repeating that pattern.

But as you continue with your POPs and your chart, you will undoubtedly experience a moment of awe, maybe ever so brief. When a sudden, unexpected bit of clarity appears, you will recognize you are in charge of stress, moodiness, and depression. You are no longer a victim. You have a choice to free yourself, now and in the future, one step at a time. This is a miracle you have created. Once you feel it the first time, you will want more. And then you will be on your way to recovery.

As you experience this new dimension, you may start to notice an occasion or two when you maintain more direct eye contact with someone because you have gained a sense of self-confidence that you didn't have before. You might gain a new awareness of nature and begin to notice trees, flowers, plants, and animals in a way you hadn't seen them before. You will begin to feel less inclined to impress others around you. You may come to understand each person is worth the same as every other person, and any status rating is fictional. Most likely, as you progress, you will lose your old personal inhibitions and find yourself more sociable. The tension you are accustomed to feeling may also start to fade away.

From a health standpoint, you will find many advantages, too. You will feel more energy and likely require less sleep.

When someone says or does something in your presence and you feel an emotional response, it's because you still believe your mind's chatter. It may take time for you to choose to believe otherwise. Until then, you may continue to have emotional times. However, if you continue practicing POPs, you will start to recognize that these bouts begin to lessen in volume and density. Eventually you will come to see that all emotional events are temporary. Each of those battles is like a cloud passing over, one at a time. I recommend you accelerate your POPs during these challenging times.

The more attention you devote to getting and staying in the present time, the quieter your mind will be.

So, you are on track. Practice your POPs, and keep adding to your chart. Congratulations. You are on your way to peace. No more preaching, because by now you know the drill: Over-thinking causes stress and depression. And POPs will get you out of it, one step at a time.

Chapter 12

My Experience with POPs

Once I started practicing, the exercises became irresistible.

It seemed as if I had everything to gain and nothing to lose.

Chapter 12

My Experience with POPs

As I developed the concept of POPs and began using them, I visualized my lungs as plastic bags that inflated and deflated as I breathed. I recognized I was "in the moment" and free of problems during that brief time, but I didn't realize why this peace was coming about. I just knew I had a phenomenal feeling of freedom.

In the past, with all my self-help study, I had experienced plenty of short periods of clarity of mind, but never a continuing, consistent peace such as I was feeling now.

Once I was on board, so to speak, there was no other place I wanted to go. I only wanted to eliminate the problematic mental streaming in my life. The exercises became irresistible. It seemed as if I had everything to gain and nothing to lose.

In the first few days, I did the exercises in a deliberate way. But in a matter of weeks, the practice became more natural. I was becoming more aware of when I was unaware. Just this realization alone was life changing. Increasing my awareness of when I was in present time has been for me a painless and monumental gain.

My Experience with POPs

And it is still that way today. As busy as I have become, I require less rest. I feel a decrease in my respiratory rate as well as a decrease in muscle tension. I am more sociable because I am less burdened with problems, which have become like vapors, thinned-out and minimized in my mind. I'm convinced the excess drama and emotion had been wearing me down day by day. But not anymore. Every day I am practicing Pieces of Peace, and daily I am becoming more and more free.

Chapter 13
Conclusion

I'm convinced the excess drama and emotion had been wearing me down day by day. But not anymore. Every day I am practicing Pieces of Peace, and daily I am becoming **more** *and* **more free.**

Chapter 13

Conclusion

I know what it's like to feel miserable, day in and day out. I know what it's like to be fearful. I know what it's like to often feel angry. I know what it's like to feel stressed, day after day.

In stark contrast, I now know what it feels like to be grateful each day, to feel energized, to feel love, and to feel hope. The magnitude of this kind of transformation is almost indescribable. But the underlying message is this: I am in charge of my own happiness, minute to minute, and so are you. The level of joy you desire is within your own grasp.

I used to think happiness had to do with "happenings." I thought if something happened that benefited me or was in my favor, it caused me to be happy, and if an event happened that was not in my favor, it caused me to be unhappy.

I am convinced this is how most of our society thinks. Many people try to gain happiness by getting some thing, such as a new, fancy house or a snazzy car. Or they might seek happiness by achieving someone else's acceptance—for instance, by helping others or doing good deeds. They might work hard to gain a promotion at work, thereby gaining higher status and respect, assuming the achievement will make them happier than before. There are countless ways to try to get a dose of happiness. They all have one common denominator: They are external pleasures of one sort or another—some circumstance or thing or person or action outside of oneself.

How does being happy feel? How long does the feeling last? Does it continue when you get up the next morning? Does it last a week, a month, or a year? Is there such a thing as permanent happiness?

If you help one person with his needs and then feel happy about your good effort, will you soon need to do more to gain more happiness? If you have a fancy car or house, will those items provide continual happiness, or will you see someone with a fancier one and feel the need to upgrade again to get another dose of happiness? Are you running faster and faster on a treadmill to find and keep happiness?

For decades I played out many of those scenarios, always with the desire to feel happiness. I thought there had to be an answer to finding lasting peace, a path to permanent happiness. I searched every possibility I could think of to find it, and I finally realized nothing external was going to do the job.

Conclusion

Becoming happy is an inside job. In a nutshell, here's what I know, and what I want to share with you so you can find happiness, too. The mind is continually chattering about things that happened in the past and things that might happen in the future. It creates a negative spin on everything, causing you worry and distress. The more you believe the stories, the unhappier you are. The only way to break free is to become aware that your thoughts are literally playing mind games with you.

Practicing Pieces of Peace consciously interrupts the flow of thoughts for brief periods, allowing you to see through the stories the mind is telling you. As you gain separation from the stories, you begin to understand that you do not have to be controlled by them. And the more you become free of the stories, the happier you will be.

Daily Logs

Daily Log

A	B	C	D	E
Entry No.	Date	% Time in Present Today	Total of Entries from Column C	Average % Time in Present (Present Moment Percentage)

Daily Log

A	B	C	D	E
Entry No.	Date	% Time in Present Today	Total of Entries from Column C	Average % Time in Present (Present Moment Percentage)

Daily Log

A	B	C	D	E
Entry No.	Date	% Time in Present Today	Total of Entries from Column C	Average % Time in Present (Present Moment Percentage)

Daily Log

A	B	C	D	E
Entry No.	Date	% Time in Present Today	Total of Entries from Column C	Average % Time in Present (Present Moment Percentage)

Daily Log

A	B	C	D	E
Entry No.	Date	% Time in Present Today	Total of Entries from Column C	Average % Time in Present (Present Moment Percentage)

Daily Log

A	B	C	D	E
Entry No.	Date	% Time in Present Today	Total of Entries from Column C	Average % Time in Present (Present Moment Percentage)

Daily Log

A	B	C	D	E
Entry No.	Date	% Time in Present Today	Total of Entries from Column C	Average % Time in Present (Present Moment Percentage)

Daily Log

A	B	C	D	E
Entry No.	Date	% Time in Present Today	Total of Entries from Column C	Average % Time in Present (Present Moment Percentage)

Notes